Original title:
Melon on My Mind

Copyright © 2025 Creative Arts Management OÜ
All rights reserved.

Author: Dexter Sullivan
ISBN HARDBACK: 978-1-80586-452-3
ISBN PAPERBACK: 978-1-80586-924-5

Luscious Moments in Time

In the garden, a treasure appears,
Round and green, it brings me cheers.
I dance with delight, the sun on my face,
Holding my bounty, what a sweet place.

A slice of sunshine, juicy and bright,
Sweet nectar drips, a sheer delight.
Friends gather 'round for the juicy share,
Laughter erupts, in the warm summer air.

Chasing the seeds that bounce and fly,
Witty remarks as they soar through the sky.
Wiping my chin with sticky delight,
These silly moments feel perfectly right.

Each bite a giggle, each taste a song,
In this fruity bliss, we all belong.
Cheers to the laughter and tasty delight,
For this lovely fruit brings pure delight!

Laughter Wrapped in Green

In the patch where laughter grows,
Round and plump, the giggle glows.
Juicy dribbles, a sticky affair,
Who knew fruit could pull a prank with flair?

Slicing wedges, a comic scene,
Seeds like jokes, burst in between.
The juice, a fountain, oh what a sight,
Even ants join the chuckles tonight!

Gentle Flow of Summer's Essence

Summer sways with vibrant cheer,
Bouncing balls of joy appear.
Each slice shared, a hearty grin,
Best served cold, the fun begins!

Fun in the sun, a sugary surprise,
Who needs a crown with these round guys?
Squirted seeds laugh as they dance,
In juicy bliss, we all take a chance!

Imagining the Garden's Kiss

In gardens lush with leafy delight,
Round green orbs bask in sunlight.
Dreams of taste, a whimsical wish,
Nature's joke, a fruity swish!

Tickling tongues with every bite,
A splash of sweetness feels just right.
Oh, nature chuckles, green and grand,
Fragrant whispers from the land!

Nature's Sweet Embrace

In fields of green where giggles play,
Round and jolly, come what may.
With each tender, juicy dance,
Life's a party, let's take a chance!

Splatters of juice, a splash of fun,
Under the sky, we laugh and run.
Nature's smile, a cheerful tease,
Life's sweet moments, like warm summer breeze!

Delight in Every Drop

In the heat of the day, oh so bright,
Juicy treasures offer pure delight.
With a splash and a squirt, laughter flows,
Chasing sunbeams where the cool breeze blows.

With each little bite, the giggles arise,
Sweetness drips down, much to my surprise.
Friends gathered round, sharing the spoils,
In this fruity oasis, we shake off our toils.

Whispers of Late Summer

Golden sunlit days, laughter rings,
Caught in a frenzy of sweet, sticky things.
Sipping the nectar of summer's best,
Chasing joy, like kids on a quest.

Silly faces, seeds flying wide,
A seed-spitting contest, oh, what a ride!
With belly laughs echoing in the air,
We feasted on sunshine, without a care.

Radiant Rind and Inner Bliss

In patches of green where shadows play,
Rinds of laughter brighten the day.
Slice after slice, we giggle and grin,
As juicy adventures swirl and spin.

Sticky fingers, we create a mess,
In a world of chaos, we feel so blessed.
Each drop of sunlight, each giggle a gift,
In the juicy realm, our spirits uplift.

In the Shade of a Fruitful Mind

Under shady leaves where the laughter's loud,
The joy of summer wraps us like a cloud.
Witty banter over slices so sweet,
With every shared joke, our happiness is fleet.

A splash of fruit punch splattering near,
We dance and we twirl, with nothing to fear.
Life's a big picnic when we're all together,
With laughter and smiles, we lighten the weather.

Rind of Reflection

In the fridge, a treasure waits,
A green orb that tempts the fates.
With each slice, joy takes its claim,
And laughter bursts like fruit champagne.

Friends gather round, it's quite the scene,
Juice-splattered shirts, what a cuisine!
We ponder life with each sweet bite,
A rind of truth in every light.

Slices of Solitude

Cutting with glee, the knife glides slow,
Each slice reveals a hidden glow.
A secret stash in the fridge awakens,
In solitude, my spirit's taken.

The chair creaks loud, my slice is vast,
This fruity treat, a joyful blast.
I laugh at thoughts that come to play,
In juicy dreams, I drift away.

Afternoon's Green Caress

Sunlight dances, casting beams,
A fruity vision, all my dreams.
Sitting pretty on a plate,
Green delight, I can't be late.

I take a bite, the world stands still,
Refreshing sweetness is my thrill.
The squirrels outside are quite bemused,
As I devour my snack, amused.

Thoughts Dripping with Flavor

Sipping juice, my thoughts cascade,
With every drop, new joys invade.
A sticky truth on my hands appears,
And laughter spills through happy tears.

Each flavor dances on my tongue,
With giggles bubbling, it's so fun.
As memories mix in this sweet spree,
I cherish moments, wild and free.

Flavors of the Warm Breeze

In the garden where the joy is clear,
Laughter floats as flavors appear.
A burst of sweetness fills the air,
Tickles my senses without a care.

Chasing shadows under sunny skies,
Cheerful chuckles, oh how time flies!
With every bite, a giggle erupts,
Life feels silly as sweetness disrupts.

Sunlight Gathered in Slices

Slices shine like little suns,
A snack that cheers and never shuns.
Each bite sings with a playful twist,
Creating giggles that can't be missed.

The colors dance in a vibrant spree,
A joyful canvas for you and me.
Juicy smiles spill as laughter flows,
In this sweet moment, anything goes.

Reflections in a Juicy World

In a world of silliness and fun,
Every drop glimmers, the laughter's begun.
Reflections of joy in a watery play,
Sipping the sweetness, what a grand day!

With each colorful splash, a joke takes flight,
Leaving behind flavors that feel just right.
In this juicy adventure, we giggle and share,
Life's joyful moments are beyond compare.

A Symphony of Sweetness

In the orchards, music softly sways,
Each note a flavor in cheerful arrays.
A symphony crafted with a wink and a grin,
As laughter plays, let the fun begin!

The sweetest melodies float through the air,
Dancing in rhythm without a care.
Join the chorus of bites and delight,
In this fruity escapade, everything's right!

A Tapestry of Flavor

In the fridge, a treasure waits,
Round and green, with juicy traits.
Slice it open, what a thrill,
Sweet delight, it fits the bill.

Seeds like stars, all in a row,
Every bite puts on a show.
Giggles rise with every taste,
A juicy game, we shan't waste.

The Essence of Sun-Drenched Days

On a lawn chair, I recline,
With a snack that feels divine.
Sunshine drips from every slice,
Laughter blooms, oh so nice!

A splash of juice, a sticky hand,
With each bite, I make a stand.
Nature's candy, pure delight,
Chasing clouds 'til the night.

Whispers in the Orchard

Underneath the leafy shade,
Daring bites of joy are made.
Friends gather, sharing a grin,
Every slice sparks joy within.

The orchard hums with laughter sweet,
Rinds are tossed, oh what a feat!
Jokes fly high like birds in flight,
Fruitful fun, it feels so right.

Cravings of a Sunny Afternoon

When the clock strikes lemonade,
I find my funky, fruity trade.
With a seed or two to spit,
Every giggle feels like it!

Picnic blankets laid with care,
Fruits are flying through the air.
Sunny faces full and bright,
Chasing joy, what pure delight!

The Orchard's Embrace

In the orchard where I roam,
Fruit is bouncing like a foam.
With every bite, a giggle springs,
Joyful laughter is what fruit brings.

Shadows dance beneath the trees,
Wobbling like a jiggly breeze.
Who knew fruit could play this way?
A fruity chuckle for the day!

Colors bright like party hats,
Silly songs for silly cats.
Oranges blush and lemons sigh,
While apples wink as they go by.

With friends we laugh till we drop,
That juicy texture makes us hop.
In the orchard's warm embrace,
We share the joy, it's quite the race!

Slice of Bliss

A slice of joy upon my plate,
In summer sun, it feels so great.
With flavors dancing, can't resist,
This fun-filled treat, I must persist!

Juicy drips with every bite,
Tickles taste buds, pure delight.
A splash of laughter in my day,
This goofy fruit is here to stay!

Each chunk's a smile, bright and bold,
Like sunny stories waiting to be told.
With friends around, we'll munch away,
In this fruity game, we laugh and play.

Careful now, don't drop the slice,
Your giggles will be worth the price.
In this sunny, juicy mess,
You'll find pure bliss — I must confess!

The Essence of Sunlight

Sunshine mixed with cheeky fun,
Bright green shades shine in the sun.
Bobbing heads and merry grins,
With each sweet bite, the laughter spins.

Chasing shadows on the ground,
In this sweetness, joy is found.
A juicy burst that makes us squeal,
Brighting our moments with zest and zeal.

With wit as sharp as any knife,
This fruit's the star of our joyful life.
Bouncing giggles from every bite,
Making our day oh-so-bright!

Silly hats and laughter rings,
Under the sun, our spirit sings.
In this bright and funny dance,
We feel the magic — it's our chance!

Nectar at Dusk

As twilight falls, fun starts to glow,
Sipping nectar, enjoying the show.
Flavor bursts by candlelight,
Hilarity grows, oh what a sight!

With every sip, we share our dreams,
In the pink dusk, laughter streams.
Sweet and silly, like a balloon,
We giggle and munch under the moon.

Who knew such fun could be so sweet?
Laughing, chasing, in a fruity feat.
With each drop, our smiles grow wide,
As the magic fruit awaits inside!

At dusk we find our happiest blend,
With nature's bounty, our silly friend.
In evening's glow, joy takes its flight,
Nectar of laughter, oh what a night!

Sweet Reflections Under the Sun

Sipping juice on a sunny day,
A sticky smile comes out to play.
Seeds in my teeth, a funny sight,
Laughing loud, my heart's delight.

Bright yellow flesh, oh what a bite,
Giggling friends, everything's right.
The summer breeze dances along,
We sing a silly, sweet summer song.

The Seed Inside My Soul

Life's a riddle, seeds 'round we toss,
Unraveled dreams, oh, what a loss!
With every grin, the laughter grows,
A world of wonders, in silly flows.

Deep in my heart, a seedling dreams,
With every laugh, a new joy beams.
Planting giggles to sprout and spry,
Watch those chuckles reach for the sky.

Summer's Lush Serenade

Under the shade, we munch and munch,
A juicy snack for our funny lunch.
Tommy slips, oh what a fall,
He lands right in the fruit-filled sprawl!

We throw seeds like wishes in air,
Aim for the birds, oh, what a dare!
Each splat and splatter brings joyful cheer,
Summer laughter that we hold dear.

Honeyed Dreams on the Horizon

With each sunrise, bright joy arrives,
Sweet as honey, my heart derives.
Days filled with giggles, pure and bright,
Chasing the sun with all my might.

In juicy moments, we sip and grin,
A sticky treasure, let the fun begin!
Laughter echoes as the flavors blend,
Our honeyed dreams, they never end.

Biting into Sunshine

A slice so bright, it gleams with cheer,
Juicy dribbles, oh so dear.
Each bite's a laugh, a giggly pool,
Sweet delight, it's the ultimate fool.

In summer's grip, it winks at me,
A testament of sticky glee.
Handfuls of taste, the burst of fun,
Why is this not the only one?

The Wonder of Ripening

Oh how you grow, in style and grace,
Sporting colors, a cheeky face.
With every day, you swell with pride,
I'm giggling as you simply abide.

A dance of textures, a playful sway,
Who knew a fruit could have such a play?
Tickling taste buds, an epic quest,
You're the punchline, you know you're blessed.

Glimmers of Citrus Bliss

A zesty wink from citrus shores,
A fruit that hides behind its doors.
With every peel, hilarity unfolds,
It's like a comedy with secrets untold.

A splash of juice splatters the air,
Oh, what a riot, without a care!
Each segment bursts with laughter bright,
A happy snack, what a delight!

Sweet Thoughts in the Shade

Dreaming under leafy crowns,
With whispers of sweetness, nobody frowns.
The fruits are gossiping, can't you hear?
Sharing secrets, tickling our ear.

In the coolness, we chuckle away,
Fruit-fueled giggles save the day.
Each nook and cranny, a treasure to find,
Oh, what a joy, this frivolous grind!

The Juicy Reverie

In the fridge, a treasure waits,
Round and green, it holds my fate.
With a grin, I grab a knife,
Sweet juice flows, oh, what a life!

Sips of sunshine, a tasty swim,
Thoughts of summer start to brim.
Caught in laughter, seeds to chew,
Oh, the joy of something new!

Chasing bites in every bite,
A giggle here, a juicy flight.
Sticky fingers, endless fun,
In my dreams, I'm on the run!

From picnic plans to silly fights,
Who will take the last one's rights?
In this world, I am the king,
With every slice, I laugh and sing!

Sun-Kissed Delights

On a plate, so bright and bold,
Sliced and laughing, truth be told.
Wedges dance with every slice,
Sunshine's laughter, oh, so nice!

Picnic tables, ants in sight,
Chasing crumbs, oh what a sight!
Juicy giggles fill the air,
Who knew fruit could be such flair?

Underneath the summer's gleam,
Lemonade flows, you know the theme.
And while we snack, the jokes take flight,
Fruity puns bring pure delight!

With every bite, the silly grows,
Can you guess where this one goes?
In my heart, a simple cheer,
For sun-kissed dreams, we hold so dear!

Thoughts Afloat in Mellow

In a bowl, they take their stand,
Plump and sweet, oh, life is grand.
Who knew thoughts could taste this good?
Sticky sweetness, my mood's renewed!

Rolling laughter, a fruity cast,
Jokes collide, they fly so fast.
Juicy giggles, left and right,
With every slice, I feel the light!

Checkered blankets, clouds above,
Nibbling softly falls in love.
A serenade of fruity cheer,
Mirth and laughter, always near!

They join the fun, the dance, the song,
Sugary thoughts can't steer me wrong.
As each bite makes spirits soar,
In fruity dreams, I always roar!

Dreaming of Honeydew

In my dreams, a sweet delight,
Crisp and fresh, in morning light.
Feeling giggles in every bite,
A silly dance, oh, what a sight!

Jokes unfold as slices gleam,
Laughing loud, we form a team.
Little bites lead to big grins,
Flavors swirl, let the fun begin!

Underneath the sunny rays,
Fruit-filled laughs fill up our days.
With every moment spent on this,
Juicy moments I surely miss!

Together, we'll take on the world,
Although we know our dreams are swirled.
As laughter echoes in the air,
Honeydew dreams, beyond compare!

A Harvest of Memories

In the field sunburnt and bold,
Laughter echoes, stories unfold.
With juicy bites and silly grins,
We share our tales of sunny wins.

Rolling to find the sweetest slice,
Who knew the hunt could be so nice?
With sticky hands and giggling crew,
The joy of summer's bright debut.

Dappled Light and Seeds

Under shady trees we play,
Chasing shadows that dance and sway.
Seeds of laughter, sprouting fun,
We race the clock till day is done.

Messy faces, laughter loud,
Sweet sunlit moments to be proud.
In our hearts, the joy will stay,
Dappled light in bright disarray.

The Smoothness of Daydreams

Floating thoughts on silky streams,
Daydreams slip like melted creams.
Whimsical wishes, all in tune,
Underneath the bright, warm moon.

Giggles burst like ripe balloons,
Each moment filled with funny tunes.
Smooth as butter, sweet as gold,
Our silly tales will never be old.

Wandering Through Summer's Bounty

Wandering paths where treasures grow,
Every step sparks fun to sow.
With every taste, a grin we share,
Sumptuous sweetness fills the air.

Chasing down the perfect bite,
Who can resist such pure delight?
In nature's garden, we all blend,
We laugh and play, our hearts transcend.

Chasing the Sweet Breeze

In the garden, I'm a dreamer,
With thoughts of summer cheer.
Fruits a-frolic in my mind,
A juicy prize draws near.

Laughter bubbles from a tree,
With every slip and dive.
I chase the wind, it tickles me,
Where the sweet fruits thrive.

A hula hoop of colors bright,
Rolling down the lane.
I trip on vines, but what a sight,
My giggles can't contain.

Sunshine dances on my face,
With splashes of delight.
In this silly, sweet embrace,
All worries fade from sight.

Orchard Dreams and Juicy Thoughts

Beneath the trees, I take a seat,
A picnic with a view.
Whispers of the orchard sweet,
A tasty dream to chew.

Bouncing blooms, they tease me so,
With aromas wafting high.
Each one eager to bestow,
A smile or a sigh.

I juggle fruits, they roll away,
Escaping from my grip.
And as I laugh, I hear them say,
"Join us for a trip!"

Together we shall frolic free,
No worries in the air.
In this orchard full of glee,
Of juicy dreams we share.

Sunbeam's Gentle Whisper

A sunbeam tickles at my nose,
With laughter on its rays.
It whispers secrets, playful prose,
In warm and sunny ways.

A dance of shadows in the glade,
I spin without a care.
With every twirl, a memory made,
Of sweetness in the air.

Comedic slips, I start to slide,
On grass as soft as pie.
The sunbeam and I, side by side,
In giggles, we both fly.

The earth a canvas, bright and bold,
Painted with delight.
In joyful tales that never grow old,
We shimmer in the light.

Tides of Sweetness

Upon the shore, I dig around,
For treasures made of cheer.
Each wave that crashes makes a sound,
Of sweetness, oh so near.

I build a tower, fruits aligned,
A castle, squishy bold.
But as I laugh, it's hard to find,
The juicy tales unfold.

Seagulls swoop with playful squawks,
They want a share, you see.
I toss them bits; they dance like clocks,
In synchronized glee.

The ocean whispers, soft and grand,
Of all things bright and fun.
With every grain of golden sand,
A new adventure's begun.

Late Summer's Embrace

In the sun, I dance with glee,
A juicy treat calls out to me.
With every bite, a burst of cheer,
Wishing this sweet time would stay near.

Laughter bubbles in the air,
Sticky fingers, without a care.
A splash of juice, a little drip,
Oh, how I love this fruity trip!

Picnic blankets laid with flair,
Friends and fun, the perfect pair.
Each wedge brings giggles and delight,
As day fades into soft twilight.

So let the summer linger long,
In this flavor-filled, funny song.
For life's too short to take it slow,
Join the fun, let sweetness flow.

Fields of Flavor

In fields where green meets golden glow,
A playful feast begins to grow.
Nature's candy, round and bright,
Harvest time brings sheer delight.

Rolling in the grass we play,
Sking-tagging as we munch away.
Seeds and laughter fill the air,
Messy faces everywhere!

Bite into laughter, slice the sun,
With every taste, the joy's begun.
Chasing dreams on summer's breeze,
Savoring flavors, feeling at ease.

Fields of joy, a fruity chase,
Life's little treasures, a sweet embrace.
With friends beside, we sing and cheer,
As laughter ripens, the end is near.

Splashes of Sweetness

Diving into a bowl so bright,
Each slice is just a tasty bite.
A splash of juice, a giggle shared,
Worry fades without a care.

Sliced and served, the party starts,
Colorful hues, pure works of arts.
As juice drips down to my chin,
I laugh and say, let the games begin!

In backyard shade, we cheers and toast,
To silly stories we love the most.
From fruity feasts we can't resist,
To friendship's sweetness, we know we're blessed.

So gather round, let's eat and play,
With splashes of sweetness, what a day!
In this fruity frenzy, we find our bliss,
Each juicy moment, a fruity kiss.

A Taste of Tranquility

Sipping sunshine from a cup,
As easy laughter fills me up.
A taste so sweet, it calms my soul,
In this moment, I feel whole.

Lying back on summer grass,
Watching clouds as they drift past.
With every flavor, life slows down,
A slice of joy, without a frown.

Underneath the laughing trees,
The world feels light, as I feel these.
With every nibble, peace I find,
In nature's bounty, sweet and kind.

So here I stay, with heart content,
In quiet bliss, there's no lament.
Just flavors dancing, softly swaying,
In this calm, my spirit's playing.

A Slice of Serendipity

In a patch so bright and green,
Lies a fruit that knows what fun means.
It dances in the summer breeze,
With seeds like confetti in the trees.

Giggling softly in the heat,
It rolls about with wobbly feet.
A traitor to the serious minds,
It swears it's sweet, defying kinds.

All my worries start to slip,
With every juicy, laughing sip.
On a plate, it takes a dive,
In a world where happiness thrives.

So slice and share this joyful sphere,
Taste its laughter, bring good cheer.
With every munch and silly grin,
We celebrate the joy within.

Sunlight Soaked Thoughts

Underneath the sunny rays,
I dream of bright and fruity days.
A ball of joy upon my plate,
Wiggling, giggling—what a fate!

Oh, how it gleams like summer joy,
A cheerful plump, a fruity toy.
Quiet moments, joyfully shared,
In each bite, no worries spared.

With laughter bubbling in my soul,
Even the clouds can't take their toll.
Peeling laughter from its rind,
Sunlight bubbles in my mind.

A squishy treat, so full of glee,
Floating on waves of jubilee.
Let's savor this bright, silly bliss,
In every juicy, happy kiss.

Dreamy Days Under the Shade

In the coolness of a leafy dome,
I find a juicy chubby poem.
A sweet delight that says, 'Take care!'
With every slice, I float on air.

Laying back, surrounded by cheer,
This treasure whispers, 'Come, my dear!'
Each little drip brings a chuckle,
Like summer dreams in joyful buckle.

Wobbly jests in the afternoon sun,
A parade of laughter, oh what fun!
With sticky fingers and silly grins,
Each bite begins where joy just spins.

So here's to days of laughter's spark,
Under the trees that leave their mark.
With a slice so round, so sweet and bright,
Turn every moment into pure delight.

The Garden's Harmony

In a garden blooming bright and wide,
A playful joy I cannot hide.
A fruit that giggles, rolls and sings,
Bringing laughter, oh what fun it brings!

With vines that stretch like silly dreams,
It teases us with juicy themes.
Chasing shadows, skipping light,
Turning munching into pure delight.

Every bite's a comedy show,
Juicy smiles in every row.
Under the sun, we laugh and play,
In this sweet garden, come what may.

So gather round, don't miss the show,
As happiness and sweetness flow.
In the garden's endless embrace,
We find our joy, a happy place.

Juicy Daydreams

In the shade of sunlit beams,
I daydream of the sweetest schemes.
A wobble here, a giggle there,
Imagining a fruit beyond compare.

Bouncing round like jelly jam,
Rolling down the hill, oh damn!
A splash of juice, a sticky kiss,
In my thoughts, it's pure bliss.

Wearing seeds like spots of fun,
I'm ready for a summer run.
With every bite, I laugh and sway,
In juicy dreams, I wish to play.

With a grin that's wide and bright,
I'll munch my way into the night.
Those dreams delight, oh what a sight,
I toast to fruit, let's take a bite!

A Slice of Summer's Whisper

A summer slice, oh what a tease,
With laughter buzzing in the breeze.
It's bright and bold, a cheerful round,
Where happiness and juice abound.

Giggles follow each juicy bite,
Spitting seeds, oh what a sight!
Sunshine drips from every rind,
In every seed, pure joy I find.

Dancing in the warm sunlight,
Each slice brings a fresh delight.
I juggle flavors, can't resist,
Such fun in every fruity twist!

So here I am, a happy fool,
With nature's candy, that's my rule.
With laughter ringing oh so sweet,
Each little bite's a tasty treat!

Green Orb of Delight

What's this orb, so round and green?
A playful sight, a jester's dream.
I dare to roll it with great flair,
Bounce and giggle, light as air!

A wink from nature, round and sweet,
It brings the joy, can't be beat!
I carve a slice, and oh, the glee,
It's joy and laughter, just for me!

Summer's burst in every bite,
Chasing worries, pure delight.
With friends around, the laughter flows,
In this green joy, my heart glows.

Every scoop's a fun-filled race,
A jolly dance, we keep the pace.
In every giggle, jest, and cheer,
This green orb brings us all right here!

Thoughts in the Patch

In a patch where sunlight plays,
I ponder sweet, juicy days.
Spinning round with each delight,
My giggles echo, oh so bright!

I'm hopping from one dream to two,
Imagining adventures, me and you.
With sticky hands and laughter loud,
In this patch, we're all so proud.

A juicy grin, who can resist?
Each happy thought, a fruity twist.
With every drop of sweetened cheer,
I gather joy, my friends draw near.

So here we sit, in nature's grace,
With chuckles and bites, a joyful race.
In this patch, I find my way,
Laughter blooms, come join the play!

Serenade of Succulence

In my bowl, a slice so round,
Its sweet juice is where joy is found.
I giggle as I take a bite,
The fruit parade feels just so right.

With every drip, my shirt's a show,
A sticky mess, but who would know?
The seeds may scatter, oh what fun,
A seed-spitting race has just begun!

Each munch brings laughter, loud and clear,
Friends all around, there's nothing to fear.
A funny face with juice on my chin,
Summer's delight, let the games begin!

So here's to bites of sweet delight,
With every chunk, the world feels bright.
A fruity joke that keeps us grinned,
In every flavor, giggles are pinned.

Refreshing Echoes

A splash of flavor hits my tongue,
The joyful sound of laughter's sung.
I chase the juice, it runs too fast,
Like silly races, what a blast!

Squirts of sweetness, here and there,
The little bites weave through the air.
I wear the fruit like a crown of cheer,
With each giggle, summer draws near.

A picnic scene, the ants are sly,
They join the feast, oh my, oh my!
With nature's sweets, we all unite,
Our belly laughs soar to the height.

Each juicy moment, we all adore,
The echoes of laughter beg for more.
With every munch, our cares do flee,
The world's a playground, wild and free.

Garden of Whimsy

In the garden, fruits abound,
Each shape and size spread all around.
A riot of colors in the sun,
A fruity feast has just begun!

I pluck a slice, so big and bright,
It wobbles and jiggles, oh what a sight!
Laughter bubbles as I take a bite,
Juice in my hair—a true delight!

The critters giggle, the bugs all cheer,
As we munch together, summer's dear.
With every taste, we feel so spry,
In this garden, let out a joyous cry!

Let's dance around with playful glee,
Let sweetness and laughter be our decree.
Each laughter shared, the heartbeat grows,
In this silly world, joy overflows.

Taste of Sunlit Days

Under the sun, the fun awaits,
With juicy bites, let's tempt our fates.
A toast to flavors, oh so bright,
In every slice, pure delight!

Laughter sprinkled on every plate,
A silly dance—can't help but gyrate.
The fruity festival brings us near,
Each taste a giggle, laughter here!

Slippery seeds take flight like dreams,
With each juicy bite, the daylight gleams.
A patchwork of joy, bold and loud,
In sunlit days, we're all quite proud.

So here's to summers, light and sweet,
With friends and fun, we're so complete.
In every laughter, life's a ball,
With quirky bites, we'll rise, we'll fall!

Rind of Serenity

In the summer sun, I roam,
With a slice in hand, I feel at home.
Juicy drips down my chin,
What a delightful way to begin!

Seeds spitting tales of yore,
Laughter echoing, who could want more?
A perfect picnic by the creek,
Nature's laughter feels so sweet!

Squirrels eyeing my tasty treat,
Are they jealous of my summer feat?
This green treasure, oh so bright,
Makes the lazy afternoons feel right!

Underneath the shady tree,
I munch away, feeling free.
With every bite, I giggle loud,
In my fruity joy, I'm proudly cowed!

Cravings for the Sunkissed

Oh, the sweetness of the day,
A burst of flavor, come what may.
My taste buds dance, what a sight,
Every bite feels so right!

Bright and sunlit on my plate,
I contemplate my fruity fate.
Sunkissed slices all around,
In this joy, I'm tightly bound!

My friends all gather, sharing cheer,
As the juice drips down, we appear!
With every giggle, a grand toast,
To this treat we love the most!

Oh, how I crave this sunshine bliss,
In each bite, an eternal kiss.
Life's so funny with this delight,
Chasing flavors, morning to night!

The Fruit of Lazy Afternoons

With a fork in hand, I begin,
In this delicious wonder, I always win.
Chilling outside, no care in sight,
Savoring nature, pure delight!

Laughter carries on the breeze,
As I make faces, do what I please.
Squishy bites under the sun,
Life's a game, and I have fun!

The world spins fast, but here I stay,
In this fruity thrill, I play all day.
No deadlines ever in this space,
Just juicy smiles on every face!

So here's to afternoons so sweet,
With every juicy, joyful treat.
In this moment, I find my way,
To bright tomorrows that always play!

Nostalgia in Every Bite

A taste that brings me back to youth,
With giggles, games, and simple truth.
Sticky fingers and happy shouts,
In a world without any doubts!

Grandma's kitchen, the air alive,
With fruity scents that help me thrive.
We'd slice it up, laughter around,
In every corner, joy was found!

Now I sit, reliving the past,
In each taste, memories are cast.
Though time may fly, and days grow old,
The joy of fruit will never fold!

So here I savor, here I delight,
With every bite, I reignite.
In sweetness wrapped, the past takes flight,
Nostalgia blooms in colors bright!

Canvas of a Summer Fantasy.

In fields where laughter floats like bees,
Bright orbs of joy hang low from trees.
With each bite, sun-drenched sweetness sings,
A juggling act that summer brings.

Splatters of juice, a sticky delight,
Giggles erupt in the warm, soft light.
A fruit parade in a vibrant hue,
Every slice tells tales anew.

Skateboards swirl on asphalt lanes,
As friends unite in fruity campaigns.
Who knew a fruit could spark such glee?
Playing tag under the big, green tree!

Memories float like seeds in the air,
Sunshine and laughter, everywhere!
Our summer canvas, wild and free,
Bursting with joy, just you and me.

Summer's Sweet Whisper

Whispers of sweetness dance in the breeze,
Fruit masks hiding in leafy trees.
A playful nibble, laughter galore,
Juicy secrets the sun has in store.

Picnics filled with absurdity bright,
Witty puns taken to new heights.
A fruit fight breaks out, oh what a scene,
Drenched in colors of gold and green!

With a squishy scoop, those giggles rise,
Chasing splats under the clear blue skies.
Everyone's grinning more than a while,
As fruit-filled moments bring out a smile!

The season's a canvas, bright and free,
Where every step feels just like a spree.
The sweet whispers echo, oh what fun,
In this fruit kingdom, we are all one!

Seeds of Daydreams

Seeds of dreams pop in midday sun,
Chasing sunshine, oh what fun!
Stumble on laughter, trip on delight,
And sticky mischief takes flight.

A splash of color, a burst of taste,
Who knew delight could travel in haste?
Squeezing joy from juicy bites,
As giggles sparkle like summer nights!

Thoughts floating like kites on a string,
In a world where happy vibes swing.
Laughter and juice, what a sweet esteem,
Each moment crafted like a daydream.

We dance through fields of sun-soaked cheer,
Every pluck of fruit draws us near.
With a wink and nod, we embrace the scenes,
In the garden of whimsical routines!

Lush Green Thoughts

Beneath a sky of the bluest blue,
Lush thoughts sprout like they always do.
Each round treasure, bright and true,
In the summer sun, a wonderful view.

With laughter echoing off every wall,
We've got our cups, let's have a ball!
Tumbling around in fields of green,
Unleashing joy, like never seen!

Sipping sweetness from nature's cup,
Up on our toes, never giving up.
Splatters of flavor guide our way,
It's a juicy trance we embrace today!

In the realm of dreams, we plant our seed,
Sun-kissed tomfoolery is all we need.
With each big bite, let's be sublime,
In this fun-filled journey of summer time!

Chill of a Cool Slice

On a scorching day, oh what a treat,
A cool slice awaits, it's nature's sweet.
With sticky fingers, I take a bite,
Refreshing joy, pure and light.

Giggles erupt with each juicy squirt,
My shirt's a canvas, the stains they flirt.
Friends gather 'round, and laughter flies,
As we share stories 'neath sunny skies.

Sipping nectar from a paper straw,
With dribbles and drops, we break the law.
The seeds become ammo for playful games,
As we aim and fire, no one feels shame.

Every juicy morsel brings pure delight,
Sun-soaked fun from morning till night.
In the backyard, it's a flavor spree,
Where each bite bursts with sweet glee!

A Drizzle of Golden Hues

Golden drops glisten, like sunshine's cheer,
From a slice so bright, it's the taste we revere.
With each juicy drip, my taste buds pirouette,
A fruit ballet, no regrets, no sweat.

A puddle of nectar on my plate,
I dive right in, I can't hesitate.
With laughter erupting, the juice takes flight,
As we feast like kings, all day and night.

The colors collide, a feast for the eyes,
Each droplet a treasure, a sweet surprise.
We wear our stains like badges of zest,
From the golden droplets, we've truly been blessed.

The title of artist, we each claim loud,
Using fruit and laughter, we're painting a crowd.
In the gallery of fun, we're the brightest hue,
Where every slice shared makes us feel brand new!

Sweet Juices of Memory

Under the sun, our laughter sings,
The sweet juices dance on carefree wings.
Childhood treasures in every bite,
Nostalgia's flavor, pure delight.

With melting smiles, we reminisce,
Every bite a former blissful kiss.
Juicy stories dribble down our chins,
As we savor the joy that the summer brings.

In patchy grass, we giggle and play,
The sticky sweetness just won't fade away.
With faces aglow, our spirits rise,
Happy memories wrapped in warm skies.

Each drip and drop a tale to share,
In every slice, memories laid bare.
With fruity laughter, we conquer the day,
In this juicy kingdom, let's forever stay!

The Color of Afternoon

Afternoon sun, casting warm rays,
In juicy realms, we lose our ways.
Laughter ripples through the grassy knoll,
As fruity flavors awaken our soul.

A splash of color on our plates,
Every bite erupts, oh, how it elates!
With sticky fingers and a grateful heart,
We play and feast, a juicy art.

While birds serenade from the leafy trees,
We sample the summer with the gentlest breeze.
Slipping and sliding, oh what a race,
The joy of fruit paints smiles on each face.

Together we tease, we laugh, we share,
As laughter and sweetness fill the air.
In the color of afternoon, we find our groove,
The perfect blend of fun and smooth!

The Weight of Juicy Thoughts

Round and plump, a thought arrives,
Squishing dreams, a taste that thrives.
Sticky fingers, laughter spills,
Wobbling joys, oh, what a thrill!

Like a secret tucked away,
Beneath the sun, it longs to play.
The weight of thoughts can feel so sweet,
A jolly tune, a cheerful beat!

In the fridge, it takes a nap,
Waiting for the perfect clap.
Slice it open, colors bright,
Juicy giggles in the light!

So here I sit, and ponder deep,
Of fruity dreams that make me leap.
With every bite, a chuckling sigh,
These juicy thoughts just never die!

Sun-Kissed Wanderlust

A ball of cheer on summer days,
Rolling laughter down the ways.
Shades on eyes, a quirky dance,
Adventure calls, let's take a chance!

Skewered dreams on wooden sticks,
Lemonade and berry tricks.
Waves of giggles, sunburned skin,
A juicy world where fun begins!

Tickled toes in sandy toes,
Where every breeze is ripe and glows.
Tropical theme in every town,
A spiral of joy that spins around!

The road is bright, the sky's aflame,
With every twist, we play the game.
A fruit-filled carousel we ride,
In shades of joy, we'll always glide!

A Garden of Whimsy

In a patch of green, giggles grow,
With wobbly fruits that steal the show.
Tiny sprites with laughter bright,
Tending whimsies day and night.

Potting joy in rainbow hues,
Sprinkling laughter like morning dew.
Each plant a joke, each bloom a jest,
In this garden, we're truly blessed!

Dancing leaves in breezy cheer,
Who knew silliness thrived right here?
Pull a carrot, find a pun,
Blooming chuckles, oh what fun!

So grab your hat and come along,
To a garden where we all belong.
With roots in joy, our hearts entwined,
In a place that's simply one of a kind!

Slices of Serendipity

Chopping joy with every slice,
Unexpected laughs, oh so nice!
Sweet surprise in each section,
Fruity whimsy's our connection.

Segments bright, a colorful feast,
Every nibble feels like a tease.
Belly laughs and rolling smiles,
Joyous moments stretch for miles!

Gathered friends, a cheerful buzz,
Sharing bites, it's simply was!
Juicy tales we love to share,
With every slice, we breathe the air!

Life is ripe with silly things,
Fun and laughter, what joy it brings!
So take a piece, and laugh with me,
In slices of sweet serendipity!

Serene Roots of Thought

In the garden of my head, things grow,
With fruits so strange, they put on a show.
A ball of green, with a grin oh so wide,
Chasing the clouds, on a flavorful ride.

In the silence of thought, they bounce with glee,
Tickling my brain like a cheeky bumblebee.
Ideas drip sweet, like nectar from trees,
I chuckle and ponder, 'Oh, what a tease!'

Melodic Slices of Joy

Slicing the laughter with juicy delight,
Every bite bursting, a taste of pure light.
Let's dance on the breeze, with flavors so bold,
As stories unfold, they never get old.

The picnic's a riot, with juice flying high,
A slippery slide as we laugh and we cry.
Chasing the sun, with a grin on my face,
Sharing sweet moments, a joyful embrace.

Dappled Dreams Among Leaves

In the shade of the tree, where giggles take flight,
Thoughts are like shadows, playful and light.
With hues of the afternoon drifting and swirled,
Each flicker of joy spins its own little world.

The fruit may be hefty, yet smiles are contagious,
As we toss them about—oh, it feels quite outrageous!
In the laughter-filled air, come join in the spree,
With nature's green jesters, forever carefree.

Warmth of the Sunlit Orchard

In the warmth of the sun, the orchard is bright,
Where giggles and textures create pure delight.
With a jolly round shape, they lounge in the sun,
Each curve tells a tale, bursting with fun.

The whispers of leaves tell secrets in jest,
As we frolic and play, life feels like a fest.
Join hands with the breeze, let the laughter fly free,
In this sunny orchard, we'll make history!

Wandering Through Orchard Skies

Beneath the sun, I prance and sway,
With fruity dreams that play all day.
The breeze whispers jokes in a fruity cheer,
As I gobble laughter, I start to steer.

In orchards bright, I skip and twirl,
Chasing giggles, oh what a whirl!
A juicy treasure hides in the leaves,
While playful thoughts dance like summer's breeze.

With polka dots on a canvas of green,
My thoughts bounce like balls; they don't care to be seen.
I stumble and trip, then burst out in glee,
For life's a circus among the cherry trees.

As the sun dips low, laughter does fade,
Still, remnants of fun keep joy remade.
Each step I take, each zap of delight,
A treasure of whimsy, oh what a sight!

Thoughts Dripping with Sweetness

I woke up one day with a giggle so grand,
Thoughts oozed like syrup, all sticky in hand.
Sipping on sunshine, oh what a bliss,
Thoughts dripped and splashed, I can't help but miss.

With every bite of that sweet, juicy bliss,
Life dances in rhythm, can't let that slip!
A sugar rush fills the air around,
As I chase silly dreams, laughter's profound.

Underneath the shade, I chuckle and snort,
Imagining flavors of life's funny court.
With every little giggle, sweet juices flow,
I bask in silliness, letting joy grow.

The world's a dessert, made tasty with glee,
Spinning round and round, like fruity confetti.
As thoughts drip down like a sweet summer song,
In my sunny orchard, where I belong!

A Taste of Sunlit Memories

Memories ring like giggles in air,
Tart and sweet, with stories to share.
Sunshine drips off each fruity delight,
As laughter wraps round, feeling just right.

Childhood echoes with a tickle of zest,
Pop! goes the moment, a fruity fest!
Chasing the colors of wild, swirling fun,
Where silliness ripens and can't be outdone.

In my whimsical world, nothing is bland,
With chuckles and sweetness that perfectly stand.
Juicy snippets of laughter swirl in my mind,
Popping like bubbles, oh blissfully blind.

As day turns to dusk, the joy holds tight,
Even the stars gather 'round for the night.
With each moonlit giggle, memory's taste,
Fruity chuckles linger, and never go to waste!

Refreshing Echoes of Green

In fields of green, where the giggles bloom,
I leap like a kid, dismissing all gloom.
Whispers of laughter float on the breeze,
Tickling the senses with playful tease.

With echoes of fruitiness, joy takes its flight,
Morning dew twinkles, oh what a sight!
Life's all about laughter, let's not be shy,
As we dance in the fields, under the wide sky.

Mischief runs wild where the sweetness flows,
In every tickle, a new giggle grows.
The taste of fresh fun is best when it's shared,
With friends all around, our hearts are bared.

So here's to the moments, both funny and bright,
When laughter and joy are the purest delight.
As echoes of green call us back for more,
Let's chase fruity dreams, there's always the door!

Fancies Bound in Green

In the garden where laughter grows,
A fruit so bright, everyone knows.
It rolls on the ground, oh what a sight,
With seeds like tiny stars in the light.

I chase it around with giggles and cheers,
As it dodges my grasp, igniting my fears.
A game of tag with a sneaky treat,
Who knew a fruit could be so fleet!

In a patch of dreams, it does reside,
With laughter and juice, the perfect guide.
I ponder how sweet life can be,
When rolling with joy sets you free.

So here's to the fun and the silly play,
With bouncing fruit leading the way.
Let's dance in the sun, with no care in sight,
For fancies like these make everything right.

Serene Bites of Daydream

Beneath a shady tree I lie,
With a slice of joy flung up high.
Each bite bursts with sweetness, oh what bliss,
A moment so perfect, I can't miss.

It tickles my tongue and makes me grin,
A fruity treasure that draws me in.
With each playful nib, I laugh and sigh,
Dreaming of solar-coated pie.

In this laughter-filled noon, time stands still,
My taste buds rejoice; they have their fill.
The sun beams down, a glimmering ray,
As I munch on my thoughts, feeling okay.

Oh, joys unexpected and silly delights,
In the world of flavors, I reach new heights.
With a wink, I savor this sun-soaked scene,
Each bite a memory, serene and keen.

Burst of Sweet Imaginings

In a world where nonsense reigns supreme,
A juicy orb becomes my theme.
It wiggles and dances, bright and bold,
Each squishy moment worth more than gold.

Tasting the summer with every chew,
It giggles in colors of greenish hue.
Who knew a fruit could be so spry?
Let's laugh together, you and I!

An explosion of flavors, a funny spree,
Like a clown in a circus, wild and free.
I juggle these bites with silly flair,
As giggles arise, floating in the air.

So gather your friends and share the fun,
With juicy morsels beneath the sun.
In a delight-filled whirl of mirth and cheer,
Let's battle with sweetness and let go of fear.

The Essence of a Sunny Moment

Sunlit afternoons bring tastes so sweet,
With juicy circles that can't be beat.
A dimpled delight, with charm in store,
Like a little sunbeam begging for more.

With every slice, a giggly cheer,
As sunshine plays in the atmosphere.
In breezy whispers, the fruit takes flight,
Creating moments of pure delight.

I dream in colors of playful shades,
With seeds like confetti in intricate braids.
So let's have a laugh, make life a game,
With fruit-filled treasures that'll never be tame.

For in the warmth of a sun-drenched day,
We savor the laughter that's here to stay.
So raise your fork, join in the spree,
In this wacky world, just you and me!

Melodies of the Garden

In the garden, laughter grows,
As fruits peek out, striking poses.
A tune of vines begins to play,
With every fruit, I sway and sway.

A slice of joy, so round and bright,
Tickles the belly, pure delight.
In sunlit patches, I will roam,
These happy treats feel like home.

Buzzing bees join in the fun,
Dancing round till day is done.
With each nibble, a giggle slips,
Joy drips down from fruity quips.

So here's to crops, both wild and neat,
Nature's snacks can't be beat.
In this garden of whims, I find,
A fruity laugh that's so well-timed.

The Sweetness We Crave

With shades of green and sunny rays,
I seek the fruit that always plays.
Beneath the leaves, a treasure lies,
It teases me with fruity sighs.

A juicy bite, oh what a thrill,
Each flavor sends a joyful chill.
In every slice, a burst inside,
As laughter echoes, I can't hide.

When friends arrive, we start to share,
Silly games and fruity dare.
Who can eat the most, they claim,
Noble quests that spark the flame.

In this sweet world, we feel alive,
With every bite, our spirits thrive.
Embracing joy, with smiles so wide,
In this sugary place, we bide.

Whispered Promises Under Leaves

Under soft shadows, whispers cling,
A juicy pledge, the joy they bring.
Secret laughter among the blooms,
Funk and sweetness fill the rooms.

Vines twist around like clowns at play,
With hues that charm and brighten day.
They promise fun in every bite,
A fruitful laugh through day and night.

As shadows stretch and twilight falls,
Frolicsome giggles fill the halls.
A game of taste, who can resist?
In fruity bliss, we coexist.

So let us gather, share the cheer,
Under the leaves, no hint of fear.
With tangled roots and laughter's glee,
We bask in sweetness, you and me.

Fruits of Nostalgia

In the orchard of my youth,
Laughter lingered, oh so smooth.
Pies and smirks with every slice,
Recalling days of pure delight.

The taste of summer, in my hand,
A fuzzy orb so close at hand.
We'd race to see who reached the tree,
Memories dance wild and free.

Tickled toes on grass so green,
Each fruit was magic, oh so keen.
Silly stories spun so wide,
In every bite, our joy resides.

So let's take a trip back in time,
Where sweet adventures still do rhyme.
Together, laughing, side by side,
In this fruity world, we abide.

www.ingramcontent.com/pod-product-compliance
Lightning Source LLC
Chambersburg PA
CBHW060121230426
43661CB00003B/277